♥

i love you mum

summersdale

I LOVE YOU MUM

Summersdale Publishers Ltd
46 West Street
Chichester
West Sussex
PO19 1RP
UK

www.summersdale.com

Printed and bound in Croatia

ISBN: 978-1-84953-978-4

Substantial discounts on bulk quantities of Summersdale books are available to corporations, professional associations and other organisations. For details contact general enquiries: telephone: +44 (0) 1243 771107, fax: +44 (0) 1243 786300 or email: enquiries@summersdale.com.

To...................................

From...............................

The moment
a child is born,
the mother is
also born.

OSHO

To describe my mother would be to write about a hurricane in its perfect power. Or the climbing, falling colours of a rainbow.

MAYA ANGELOU

It may be possible to gild
pure gold, but who can make
his mother more beautiful?

MAHATMA GANDHI

♥

My mother is the bones of
my spine, keeping me
straight and true.

KRISTIN HANNAH

Love as powerful as your mother's for you leaves its own mark.

J. K. ROWLING

A mother always
has to think twice,
once for herself and
once for her child.

SOPHIA LOREN

Motherhood: all love
begins and ends there.

ROBERT BROWNING

There is such a special sweetness in being able to participate in creation.

PAMELA S. NADAV

I think you are
pretty much
perfect in
every way!

Mothers hold their
children's hands for a
short while, but their
hearts forever.

ANONYMOUS

My mother had a slender, small body, but a large heart – a heart so large that everybody's joys found welcome in it, and hospitable accommodation.

MARK TWAIN

♥

She encouraged
me to be confident
and enjoy life.

CHARLIZE THERON
ON HER MOTHER

Men are what their mothers made them.

RALPH WALDO EMERSON

Successful mothers are not the ones that have never struggled. They are the ones that never give up, despite the struggles.

SHARON JAYNES

A mother's love is whole
no matter how many
times it's divided.

ANONYMOUS

I realised that when you look at your mother, you are looking at the purest love you will ever know.

MITCH ALBOM

A mum's hug lasts long after she lets go.

ANONYMOUS

The best academy,
a mother's knee.

JAMES RUSSELL LOWELL

God's most extraordinary
work is most often done
by ordinary people in
the seeming obscurity
of a home and family.

NEAL A. MAXWELL

Thank you for teaching me you can be both strong and gentle.

Mother is the one we count on for the things that matter most of all.

KATHARINE BUTLER HATHAWAY

It seems to me
that my mother was
the most splendid
woman I ever knew.

CHARLIE CHAPLIN

A mother's happiness is like a beacon, lighting up the future but reflected also on the past in the guise of fond memories.

HONORÉ DE BALZAC

[Motherhood is]
heart-exploding,
blissful hysteria.

OLIVIA WILDE

We are born of love; love is our mother.

RUMI

Being a mother is hard
and it wasn't a subject
I ever studied.

RUBY WAX

My mother is the most supportive mother in the world, she's magical.

VIN DIESEL

♥

For the hand that rocks
the cradle is the hand
the rules the world.

WILLIAM ROSS WALLACE

Thank God for your mother.

DAVID SELZNICK

A boy's best friend
is his mother.

JOSEPH STEFANO

Where there is a
mother in the home,
matters go well.

AMOS BRONSON ALCOTT

I can do
anything
because I've
got you by
my side.

For we think
back through
our mothers
if we are
women.

VIRGINIA WOOLF

You make sacrifices to become a mother, but you really find yourself and your soul.

MARISKA HARGITAY

I am truly my
mother's son.

DAVID GEFFEN

♥

There was never
a great man who had
not a great mother.

OLIVE SCHREINER

Of all the roles I've played, none has been as fulfilling as being a mother.

ANNETTE FUNICELLO

Any child can tell you the
sole purpose of a middle
name is so he can tell when
he's really in trouble.

DENNIS FRAKES

Having children just puts
the whole world into
perspective. Everything
else just disappears.

KATE WINSLET

Mothers and their children are in a category all their own. There's no bond so strong in the entire world.

GAIL TSUKIYAMA

I am lucky to have a mum with such a great sense of humour.

Motherhood is a choice
you make every day, to put
someone else's happiness
and well-being ahead
of your own.

DONNA BALL

I am here. I brought
my whole self to you.
I am your mother.

MAYA ANGELOU

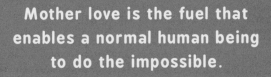

Mother love is the fuel that
enables a normal human being
to do the impossible.

MARION C. GARRETTY

My mother is a walking miracle.

LEONARDO DICAPRIO

Any mother could perform
the jobs of several air traffic
controllers with ease.

LISA ALTHER

Blessed is a mother
that would give up part
of her soul for her
children's happiness.

SHANNON L. ALDER

Where there is love,
there is life.

MAHATMA GANDHI

The most beautiful word on the lips of mankind is the word 'mother'.

KAHLIL GIBRAN

The daughter prays;
the mother listens.

AMANDA DOWNUM

There is nothing as sincere
as a mother's kiss.

SALEEM SHARMA

I can imagine no
heroism greater
than motherhood.

LANCE CONRAD

Mum, you're
my favourite
person.

Mothers possess a
power beyond that of a
king on his throne.

MABEL HALE

Our mothers always remain the strangest, craziest people we've ever met.

MARGUERITE DURAS

She rejoiced as only mothers can in the good fortunes of their children.

LOUISA MAY ALCOTT

Mothers are endowed with a love that is unlike any other love on the face of the earth.

MARJORIE PAY HINCKLEY

I wondered if my smile
was as big as hers.
Maybe as big. But
not as beautiful.

BENJAMIN ALIRE SÁENZ
ON HIS MOTHER

If you knew how great
is a mother's love, you
would have no fear.

J. M. BARRIE

♥

There is a power that
comes to women when
they give birth.

SHERYL FELDMAN

A mother's arms are made of tenderness and children sleep soundly in them.

VICTOR HUGO

Mother is the heartbeat
in the home; and without
her, there seems to
be no heart throb.

LEROY BROWNLOW

Children keep us in check.
Their laughter prevents our
hearts from hardening.

QUEEN RANIA OF JORDAN

Being a full-time mother
is one of the highest
salaried jobs... since the
payment is pure love.

MILDRED B. VERMONT

Thank you for the example you set me every day.

The art of mothering is
to teach the art of
living to children.

ELAINE HEFFNER

Mothers always know.

OPRAH WINFREY

♥

My mother has always
been my emotional
barometer and
my guidance.

EMMA STONE

In a child's eyes, a mother is a goddess.

N. K. JEMISIN

A mother is the truest
friend we have.

WASHINGTON IRVING

The successful mother
sets her children free
and becomes more free
herself in the process.

ROBERT J. HAVIGHURST

All that I am, or hope
to be, I owe to my
angel mother.

ABRAHAM LINCOLN

Anyone who
doesn't miss
the past never
had a mother.

GREGORY NUNN

She may scold you for the little things, but never for the big ones.

HARRY S. TRUMAN

Love is a
great beautifier.

LOUISA MAY ALCOTT

A mother's hug
is like a warm
cup of tea on
a rainy day.

I thought my mum's whole purpose was to be my mum. That's how she made me feel.

NATASHA GREGSON WAGNER

All mothers are rich
when they love
their children.

MAURICE MAETERLINCK

It is to decide forever to have your heart go walking around outside your body.

ELIZABETH STONE,
ON MAKING THE DECISION
TO HAVE A CHILD

The best and most beautiful
things… cannot be seen or
even touched. They must
be felt with the heart.

HELEN KELLER

I cannot tell you how much I owe to the solemn word of my good mother.

CHARLES HADDON SPURGEON

Being deeply loved by someone gives you strength, while loving someone deeply gives you courage.

LAO TZU

Children are not a
distraction from more
important work. They are
the most important work.

JOHN TRAINER

♥

No language can express
the power, and beauty,
and heroism, and majesty
of a mother's love.

EDWIN H. CHAPIN

I think my life
began with
waking up
and loving my
mother's face.

GEORGE ELIOT

My mother... she is
beautiful, softened at
the edges and tempered
with a spine of steel.

JODI PICOULT

All that I am my
mother made me.

JOHN QUINCY ADAMS

You are
irreplaceable.

One is loved
because one
is loved. No
reasons are
needed for
loving.

PAULO COELHO

I want my children to
have all the things I couldn't
afford. Then I want to
move in with them.

PHYLLIS DILLER

Love is being
stupid together.

PAUL VALÉRY

♥

Children and mothers
never truly part
Bound in the beating of
each other's hearts.

CHARLOTTE GRAY

She was the best of all mothers, to whom, for body and soul I owe endless gratitude.

THOMAS CARLYLE

She was of the stuff of which great men's mothers are made. She was... hated at tea parties, feared in shops and loved at crises.

THOMAS HARDY

Mothers are all
slightly insane.

J. D. SALINGER

Sing out loud in the
car even, or especially,
if it embarrasses
your children.

MARILYN PENLAND

You lift
my spirits.

Stories first heard standing
at a mother's knee are
never wholly forgotten.

GIOVANNI RUFFINI

Motherhood in all its
guises and permutations is
more art than science.

MELINDA M. MARSHALL

♥

A good mother is
irreplaceable.

ADRIANA TRIGIANI

The only love
that I really
believe in is
a mother's
love for
her children.

KARL LAGERFELD

No man is poor who
has a Godly mother.

ABRAHAM LINCOLN

My mother made a brilliant impression upon my childhood life. She shone for me like the evening star.

WINSTON CHURCHILL

A mother is not a person
to lean on, but a person to
make leaning unnecessary.

DOROTHY CANFIELD FISHER

Sweater, n.: garment worn by child when its mother is feeling chilly.

AMBROSE BIERCE

Sometimes the strength
of motherhood is greater
than natural laws.

BARBARA KINGSOLVER

Pregnancy and motherhood
are the most beautiful and
significantly life-altering events
that I have ever experienced.

ELISABETH HASSELBACK

The greatest love is a
mother's; then a dog's;
then a sweetheart's.

POLISH PROVERB

No influence is so powerful as that of the mother.

SARAH JOSEPHA HALE

There is a point at which
you aren't so much mum
and daughter as you are
adults and friends.

JAMIE LEE CURTIS

I got my figure back
after giving birth. Sad,
I'd hoped to get
somebody else's.

CAROLINE QUENTIN

I wouldn't
swap you
for anything
in the world.

Heaven is at the feet of mothers.

ARABIC PROVERB

A mother's arms are
more comforting than
anyone else's.

DIANA, PRINCESS OF WALES

Children are the
anchors that hold a
mother to life.

SOPHOCLES

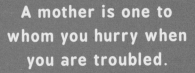

A mother is one to
whom you hurry when
you are troubled.

EMILY DICKINSON

To a child's ear, 'mother' is magic in any language.

ARLENE BENEDICT

One good
mother is
worth a
hundred
school
masters.

GEORGE HERBERT

There is no way to be a
perfect mother, and a million
ways to be a good one.

JILL CHURCHILL

Becoming a mother
makes you realise you
can do almost anything
one-handed.

ANONYMOUS

I appreciate
everything you
do for me.

Mother – that was the bank
where we deposited all
our hurts and worries.

THOMAS DE WITT TALMAGE

Mother is the name of
God in the lips and hearts
of little children.

WILLIAM MAKEPEACE THACKERAY

♥

Motherhood has a
very humanising effect.
Everything gets reduced
to essentials.

MERYL STREEP

Biology is the least of what makes someone a mother.

OPRAH WINFREY

There is no role in life
more essential and more
eternal than that of
motherhood.

M. RUSSELL BALLARD

The quickest way for
a parent to get a child's
attention is to sit down
and look comfortable.

LANE OLINGHOUSE

Love is what
makes you smile when
you are tired.

PAULO COELHO

A mother's love for her child is like nothing else in the world.

AGATHA CHRISTIE

Who is it that loves me and will love me forever with an affection which no chance, no misery, no crime of mine can do away? It is you, my mother.

THOMAS CARLYLE

Beautiful as was mamma's face, it became incomparably more lovely when she smiled, and seemed to enliven everything about her.

LEO TOLSTOY

♥

**Mother's love is peace.
It need not be acquired,
it need not be deserved.**

ERICH FROMM

A mum is a friend who will never leave you.

If love is sweet as a flower,
then my mother is that
sweet flower of love.

STEVIE WONDER

I believe the choice to become a mother is the choice to become one of the greatest spiritual teachers there is.

OPRAH WINFREY

Mum always says the right thing. She always makes everything better.

SOPHIE KINSELLA

Most mothers are instinctive philosophers.

HARRIET BEECHER STOWE

I love my mother as the trees love water and sunshine – she helps me grow, prosper and reach great heights.

TERRI GUILLEMETS

God could not be
everywhere, so he
created mothers.

JEWISH PROVERB

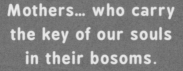

Mothers… who carry
the key of our souls
in their bosoms.

OLIVER WENDELL HOLMES SR

Mothers are the heart of any household.

HELENA BONHAM CARTER

Acceptance, tolerance, bravery, compassion. These are the things my mum taught me.

LADY GAGA

A father's goodness is
higher than a mountain,
a mother's goodness
deeper than the sea.

JAPANESE PROVERB

You're a mum
in a million.

Being a mother has made my life complete.

DARCEY BUSSELL

I know enough to know
that when you're in a
pickle... call mum.

JENNIFER GARNER

I hope they're still
making women
like my mother.

JOE LOUIS

♥

There's nothing like
a mama-hug.

TERRI GUILLEMETS

If you have a mum, there is nowhere you are likely to go that a prayer has not already been.

ROBERT BRAULT

Keep love in your heart...
The consciousness of loving
and being loved brings a
warmth and richness to life
that nothing else can bring.

OSCAR WILDE

Ultimately love
is everything.

M. SCOTT PECK

A mother understands
what a child does
not say.

ANONYMOUS

When a
child needs
a mother
to talk to,
nobody else
but a mother
will do.

ERICA JONG

Motherhood is at its best when the tender chords of sympathy have been touched.

PAUL HARRIS

If I know what love is,
it is because of you.

HERMANN HESSE